MW00941096

I DON'T KNOW HOW TO STOP

Naida M. Parson, Ph.D.

WESTBOW
PRESS®
A DIVISION OF THOMAS NELSON
& ZONDERVAN

Scripture quotations marked (NIV) are taken from the Holy Bible, New International Version®, NIV®. Copyright © 1973, 1978, 1984, 2011 by Biblica, Inc.™ Used by permission of Zondervan. All rights reserved worldwide.

Scripture quotes marked (KJV) are taken from the King James Version of the Bible.

This book is a work of non-fiction. Unless otherwise noted, the author and the publisher make no explicit guarantees as to the accuracy of the information contained in this book and in some cases, names of people and places have been altered to protect their privacy.

WestBow Press books may be ordered through booksellers or by contacting:

WestBow Press
A Division of Thomas Nelson & Zondervan
1663 Liberty Drive
Bloomington, IN 47403
www.westbowpress.com
1 (866) 928-1240

Because of the dynamic nature of the Internet, any web addresses or links contained in this book may have changed since publication and may no longer be valid. The views expressed in this work are solely those of the author and do not necessarily reflect the views of the publisher, and the publisher hereby disclaims any responsibility for them.

Any people depicted in stock imagery provided by Thinkstock are models, and such images are being used for illustrative purposes only. Certain stock imagery © Thinkstock.

ISBN: 978-1-5127-8622-4 (sc)
ISBN: 978-1-5127-8623-1 (e)

Library of Congress Control Number: 2017907459

Print information available on the last page.

WestBow Press rev. date: 07/24/2017

Dedication Page

This book is dedicated, of course to my mentor, pastor, coach, companion, teacher, partner and best friend, Jesus Christ. To my inner circle: daughter Ericka, sister best friend Regina, and best friends Angie and Shon, I thank you for your support and for never giving up on me. I know I am loved and that is because you all manage to make that plain every day. To my Spock (StarTrek), and my Cyrus (Scandal), my executive assistant Tara Trass—nothing gets done without you. Thank you for being in on every page. To my trainer and friend Sharonda, we are in this together. To Linda, thanks for keeping me on track. To my mother who passed down excellence and a way with words, I am honored to be your child. To the Family, I love you! New Antioch, you are the best!

This book is mostly dedicated to everyone who has struggled with sin, habits, behaviors and attitudes. This book is for you!

Table of Contents

Introduction

I was watching an Oprah Winfrey show on obesity in young women, particularly teenage girls. One of the teenagers was in the depths of depression, self-loathing, and hopelessness. As she told her story, my heart was engulfed by more than sympathy, empathy, and/or compassion. What I felt was total and absolute identification. I knew that helplessness. I knew that hopelessness. I knew that self-loathing...that self-hatred...and maybe so do you.

She continued to cry and tell her story of addiction to food. She knew it was stealing her life from her, both the quality of her life, and ultimately her longevity. She was so disturbed by her obesity she stated, "I would rather die than be fat." She hated her body. She hated her behavior. She hated herself for what she was doing. Then they showed another clip of this same girl. She was not exercising. She was not in a counseling session, or even a Weight Watchers meeting. They showed a clip of her stuffing a huge chilidog in her mouth, with more food on the table in front of her ready to be devoured. As she was eating voraciously, she looked into the camera and said, "I don't know how to stop."

This statement resonates with all who have dealt with a habit, a sin, a destructive behavior, or an addiction. It may be sexual misbehavior. It may be alcohol, cigarettes, illegal drugs, or prescription drugs. Perhaps it is your non-chemical drug of choice like pornography, gambling, food, gossip, or shopping. It could be a behavior that causes your relationships to deteriorate like anger, violence, need for control, or verbal abuse. This book is about any behavior you do not know how to stop. It is, more specifically, a book for those who believe it is God's will for His children to be healthy, happy, and holy. As the beloved John wrote in III John 2, "I would that you prosper and be in health even as your soul prospers." For so many of us, even those who have been born again, there are habitual behaviors in our lives that compromise our health, diminish our happiness, and in the case of repetitive sin, contaminate our holiness.

I am one who believes that God's power can and will produce, in anybody who is willing, complete and total freedom over destructive, unholy, ungodly, and unhealthy behaviors. There is a way to be free. There is a way to change. There is a way to live holy. I believe that God can change a man. I believe that God can change a woman. I believe that God can change ANYBODY! I believe that old things can pass away, and that all things can become new. (2 Corinthians 5:17 KJV)

I believe that God is able to keep us from falling and present us faultless before the presence of His Glory (Jude 24 KJV). I believe God is able to forgive our sins and cleanse us from all unrighteousness (I John 1:9 KJV). You can, and I declare by faith that you will, break every bad habit and every destructive behavior that has infiltrated your life. There is a way to stop.

To illustrate the truths presented in this book, I have constructed four fictitious stories. These individuals do not exist. They are composites of how addictive habits, destructive behaviors, and improper attitudes are formed. The scenarios don't describe any particular person. They describe a process. The people do not exist, and any similarities to any one person's story is not intentional, but not impossible. I pray that we all see ourselves in these stories and that we simply add our own details. Our childhood experiences, adult choices, and initial reactions are the materials used for the weapon that has been formed against us by the enemy of our souls. But, as the Bible declares, the weapon will not prosper. It won't work. You can be free. You can stop.

By the way, the final story in the book is true. It is mine.

CHAPTER 1

You Know How It Is

For the flesh desires what is contrary to the Spirit, and the Spirit what is contrary to the flesh. They are in conflict with each other, so that you are not to do whatever you want. (Galatians 5:17)

We know that the law is spiritual, but I am unspiritual, sold as a slave to sin. I do not understand what I do. For what I want to do, I do not do, but what I hate I do. (Romans 7:14-15)

So I find this law at work in me: Although I want to do good, evil is right there with me. For in my inner being I delight in God's law, but I see another law at work in me, waging war against the law of my mind and making me a prisoner of the law of sin at work within me. What a wretched man I am! Who will rescue me from this body that is subject to death? (Romans 7:21-24)

Y ou know how it is. You are in your car on the way to what is sure to be a sexual encounter with a person to whom you are not married. It is not what you want, but your body is aching for it. You feel the shame and the regret already, but your mind is filled with the pleasurable thought of it. Your lustful desire torments you, and you know by experience that the torment is not going to stop until you give in. Your spirit is grieved as you argue with yourself. It is already done in your heart. It was a done deal before you even hung up the phone. It was a done deal when you went to bed the night before with thoughts of the pleasure of making love, and satisfying the craving in your flesh. So you are driving over there, even with the deep sadness in your spirit that grows with every remembrance of your commitment to Christ. It grows with every recollection of the regret and the guilt you felt the last time you fell. You want to turn around, but you are even more afraid of the fight you will have with your body if you do—the torment, the longing, the desire, and the "no peace" until the body is satisfied. As you pull up in front of the place, you excitedly, yet hesitantly, put the struggle out of your mind with one last thought, "I don't know how to stop."

You know how it is. After a long stressful week, your body craves its Friday night treat. You watch one adult movie after another. You tell yourself that after this one, you are going to turn it off. Then you watch the next one. You relieve not only your sexual tension, but also the tension of the entire week. Then you decide to watch one more. You should shut it down. You should repent, but you don't, and before you know it, the sun is up and you have watched pornography all night long. Now the Internet crosses your mind, and as you head over to your computer for the next round, you say to yourself, "I don't know how to stop."

You know how it is. You lost your phone bill money in the casino already. You know you need to quit before it gets worse, but you stay a little longer. Now you have lost the power bill money, and you are forced to stay and win it back, or at least try. You did win it back! Now you are even. It is time to leave. No harm, no foul. Then again, your luck is turning now, so you stay even longer and lose all of it, and more, until all that is left is the rent money. You need to get out of there, but that would mean going home with just the rent money left. You won it all back before, so as you get set for another round knowing it is time to go (because you have done this before, and lost everything before, more than once, more than twice), you say to yourself, "I don't know how to stop."

You know how it is. They have made you so angry! You know that cussing and screaming is not productive, but you have to get this off your chest. So you keep saying hurtful things, and so do they. Now you have the advantage, so you drive the argument more aggressively. You know it's not good for the relationship. You know you are saying things you cannot take back. You know your mouth is destroying your marriage, ripping your family apart, jeopardizing your job, and ruining your friendships. You consistently get into these altercations. "This is not communication," you think to yourself, "but, I don't know how to stop."

You know how it is because, if you are reading this book, you most likely are dealing with something you don't know how to stop. Either you, or someone you know, is struggling...wanting to change...wanting to be free. Wanting to get rid of a habit, a behavior, an attitude, or an emotion. Some of you *want* to stop, because it is a sin, and your repetitive failure to change is not pleasing to God. Some of you *need* to stop, because your behavior is destroying your health, your self-esteem, or your dream. Some of you know that if you do not stop this, whatever your "this" may be, you will lose your marriage, your job, your financial standing, or even your life. Some others of you have received the call of God to a certain ministry, but cannot walk in integrity until you stop "this." Of course, therapy is an option. Long hours of counseling and behavior modification would help, and perhaps, end your cycle. Going into your childhood to understand how the habit, behavior, or desire developed, or what the behavior is covering up, has been a technique I have used throughout my career. The behavior could be generational, or simply part of the weapon formed against you by the demons assigned to you by the devil. In that case, spiritual warfare would be the way to go. Molestation, rape, abuse, family dysfunction, genetics, environment, predisposition, and childhood experiences all may have gone into the development of your particular issue. There are multiple ways to combat it depending on how you got into it in the first place.

All of the above are long books within themselves and are important to explore. However, I have found that no matter where the issue comes from, and how well you understand the spiritual, psychological, and physical aspects of it; after you have done everything from medication, to surgery, to therapy, to spiritual warfare, the life changing process you will find in these next few pages still must be followed, and maintained, to experience lasting change. These steps will work with, or without, every other thing you may try. The process is both revelation and plainly seen application of the Word of God.

You don't have to settle for struggle. There is complete freedom in the Word of God, in the power of God, in the Blood of Jesus, and in the indwelling of the Holy Spirit. In the church I grew up in, we called it "total deliverance." That means that you can be so free from an old habit, or behavior, that there is no relapse. Total and complete deliverance is God's best, and here in these pages, He offers you His best.

Salvation is called the all-inclusive word of the gospel. It means freedom, healing, wholeness, rescue, deliverance, forgiveness of sin, transformation, safety, peace, and life eternal. Because you are saved, this freedom belongs to you. There is a way to stop, and these words of life are in this book. If you are not saved, but you do believe in Jesus Christ, say the following prayer with me so that you can begin this journey as a true son or daughter of God; as a true Christian. Better yet, why don't we all say it anyway just in case!

"Jesus, I believe in you. I believe you are the Son of God and that you died on the cross for me, which paid for all of my wrong-doing (sins). Now, I give you my life. Come into my heart. Forgive me for everything I have done wrong. I admit I have been a sinner. I accept you into my heart, and I give you permission to change my life. I will live for you for the rest of my life. Thank you for saving me. Amen (so be it)."

If you believed, and meant that prayer in your heart, you are saved and should feel an internal change. This book will help you keep that change and break every bad habit you may have. Chances are, though, that you picked up this book because you are already saved, and you are still having trouble stopping destructive behaviors. You know what it is to struggle, and falter, and fail. Now you will know what it is to be free. You will know how to stop. It's as simple as one, two, three, four, five: Conviction, Conversion, Connection, Correction, and Conclusion.

CHAPTER 2

Conviction
Do You Believe It Is Wrong?

Lyla was a church girl. She was the daughter of one of the ministers who assisted the pastor. She was always the gifted one who was not only involved in every youth event of the church, but was usually the star. She could act, dance, sing, and speak. She was bright and very verbal. She often challenged her Sunday school teachers and questioned everything, from Santa Claus to the virgin birth, from the time she was old enough to form the questions. Many of the things she was taught growing up just did not make sense to her, so when she became old enough to sneak away from her strict parents, she tried everything she thought was interesting in the world.

Drinking, marijuana, and premarital sex all became part of her experimentation. She had no doubt that God was real; she just questioned whether God actually condemned her for what she was doing. One night, she was arrested for driving under the influence of alcohol and was forced into treatment as part of a plea-bargain. The whole time she was in treatment, she argued every point, and never was convinced that she was doing anything wrong. It was wrong to drive drunk, but not to drink. After all Jesus, and all the disciples, and even the Virgin Mary, drank wine. There was no convincing her, even after her third DUI, that she was out of control, or that drinking alcohol was something that was not God's will for her life. Now she was facing jail time. Her last drunken drive hurt two passengers, and although she was released until her court date, this thing had gotten serious.

Very stressed and depressed, she did what she always did when she needed to relax. She went to her favorite lounge and ordered her favorite drink, which was nothing near what Jesus, the disciples, and the Virgin Mary drank. She sat there with her drink in her hand, and her heart broken over the people she had hurt, and then did something she had stopped doing a long time ago. She got honest with herself and her God. She began to pray, admitting to God that all of her arguments about drinking were only a cover for the fact that she did not know how to stop. She got a glimpse of herself in a mirror, putting the drink to her mouth, and then it happened. She got a deep feeling of regret and remorse about her behavior. For the first time since she walked out of church years before, Lyla felt conviction. She was wrong, and she knew it in a way she had never known it before. Conviction.

Do you really believe that what you are doing is wrong? Few people will ever truly stop a behavior without a sense of conviction. It is the necessary first step for those who struggle. There may be some who just lose the desire for something and don't know why, but if you are struggling with a repetitive sin or destructive behavior, you will need a conviction.

Conviction is a strong persuasion or belief. It is being convinced of your error and compelled to admit the truth. Biblically, conviction goes deeper than being convinced. When the bible speaks of conviction, it is described as being "pricked to the heart." That means a nagging, sharp feeling of remorse, regret, and/or sorrow. Conviction is an anguish, or grief, at the wrong that you are doing. Many people are convinced of their wrong, but they are not convicted.

Do you have anguish about what you are doing? Does it feel like sin to you? Does it hurt you that your behavior hurts God? Maybe you feel bad, but do you feel pricked in your heart? This is more than your conscience. It's deeper than that. It's a deep hurtful feeling of regret. It's not just an opinion that this thing is wrong, or ungodly, or even just unwise. As the saying goes, "opinions are what men hold, but convictions are what hold men." When you are convicted, it leads to repentance.

According to Acts 2:37, when the crowd in Jerusalem heard the word spoken by the apostles, they were pricked to their heart and they said, "What shall we do?" Peter replied to them, "repent and be baptized." Repentance is the correct response to conviction. Repentance—not apology. When you are convinced that something you did is wrong, you apologize. When you are convicted, you repent.

Repentance is a change of heart, mind, and direction. Conviction motivates you to change. It's when you hate the way sin makes you feel. Doing it over, and over, again brings you to sorrow. You just cannot continue and be happy. You no longer see it as a good thing. Your body may still enjoy the activity, but something about it pricks your heart, and you want it out of your life. You most likely will never stop sinning, misbehaving, or messing up if you do not feel a conviction.

Maybe the problem with your particular issue is that you don't think it is all that wrong. Maybe you only want to quit because other people think it is wrong. Perhaps your pastor preached a sermon, or your parent, or spouse had a long talk with you about it. Maybe your wife wants you to stop smoking for your health, or your children are hurt by your multiple affairs and you feel bad about the effect on them. Maybe you were arrested for driving under the influence, and that has you thinking about not drinking at all anymore. Is it your position in your church that is giving you the motivation to address your behavior, so you can walk in integrity?

All of those are great reasons to stop, however, none of those will hold you when you are being heavily tempted. When the pressure is on, and you are being bombarded with the thought and the opportunity to engage in the activity you are trying to stop, you will need conviction. When you are stressed, or tired, or angry, the fact that other people want you to stop will not hold you. You have to have a deep cutting sense of wrong. There must be a painful regret about what you are doing.

Without conviction it is too easy to do it again and just say, "Forgive me, Lord." "I'm going to go ahead and do this for now, forgive me Lord." "You know my heart." "I am just a poor sinner saved by grace." "His mercy is new every morning, so Lord, just let me make it to the morning!" The demons assigned to you will help convince you it's not that bad. You have failed before, and God forgave you every time. Other people are doing it, and getting away with it. It's too hard to fight right now. Try again next time. No one is perfect. You deserve this. You don't feel like fighting today.

Let me park right here. As I said, the demons assigned to you (we may call it the devil, but most of us will never face the devil himself because he is not omnipresent) will persuade you to fall to the temptation. They will play down the consequences, play up God's mercy, convince you that you cannot withstand the torture of desire, and tell you that you will most likely get away with it. Then, after you give in, the same demons will hit you with an overwhelming feeling of condemnation, and depending on how "bad" the sin was, you may go into deep depression and begin to hide from God.

You won't want to pray, or worship, or even go to church on Sunday. You may feel self-hatred, anger, and severe disappointment. While you are down, you will be presented with the temptation again. Of course, by that time you are living on the corner of "what's the use" and "might as well." This starts a cycle of sin and failure, and is the devil's recipe for a backslidden condition. Realize, at this point, he is not trying to just get you to sin, he is after your destiny, your influence, and your power against his kingdom.

I parked to explain this because there is a difference between conviction and condemnation. The bible teaches that there is no condemnation to those who are in Christ Jesus (Romans 8:1). As Christians, we are to confess our sins knowing that God is faithful and just to forgive our sins and cleanse us from our unrighteousness (1 John 1:9). Before you sin, you should feel a conviction. You know in your heart that this behavior is not the right thing to do. Conviction pushes you into agreement with God. It is a prick to the heart. It is a strong emotion. But, it is not condemnation that pushes you away from God and into emotional torment, self-loathing and lowered self-esteem.

A simple distinction between the two is that conviction is what you feel from the Holy Spirit before, during, and sometimes (but preferably not) after you have sinned or experienced a failure or a fall. Condemnation is what you feel from the demons after you sin, fail, or fall. Both feelings may cross over before and after a temptation, but be careful not to fall prey to the psychological ploys of condemnation, and find yourself in a cycle of sadness, failure and repetition of the behavior. When, or if, you fall, never run from God. Run to Him! His compassions fail not. They are new every morning, and they work pretty well in the afternoon and evening, too. God has already forgiven your sins because of the shed blood of Jesus Christ, Who has paid the price for sins we haven't even committed yet. There was no gasp in heaven when you sinned. You did not take God by surprise. So there is no need to waste time and energy in condemnation. Run swiftly back to God, and repent for your wrongdoing. Do not let condemnation push you away from God. Do not let the shame and guilt torment you, and make you an easy prey for another temptation and failure.

Conviction is not condemnation, but you do need conviction. It is difficult to truly stop a behavior until you feel a conviction. You must believe the behavior is wrong, or at least that it is wrong for you. You must have a conviction that this is not God's will for your life. You must believe that this thing is not pleasing to the Lord to the point that it pricks your heart, and you cannot be comfortable living with this in your life.

For some of you reading this book, the problem is that you really don't believe that what you are doing is wrong. Do you really believe that smoking tobacco or marijuana is wrong for you? Do you really believe that sexual activity outside of marriage is sinful? Do you really believe that profanity, or drinking alcohol, or gluttony, or gossiping, is wrong for you to do? This book is not designed to convince you of what I might think is sinful. This is a book for those who know what behaviors they personally need to stop. It is for those who are wrestling with habits, attitudes, or behaviors that are destroying their lives, and they want to stop them. They want to stop because they know it is wrong for their future, their health, their spirituality, their relationships, their purpose, or their destiny.

The bible says that if you know to do something that is right or good and you don't do it, to you it is a sin (James 4:17, KJV). The bible also says, in Romans 14, that there are some things that may not be sinful for others, but could be sinful for you. It goes on to say that anything that is not done in absolute faith, in confidence that it is right, is a sin for you to do. Is it destructive to you, your family, your health, or your witness to others? Does it have more power over you than you have over it? Is it a stronghold in your life? Then it is a sin. You can't take it from me, however. If you really want to stop, you have to have your own conviction.

Well, how do I get that? I'm glad you asked that question! Conviction comes by the Holy Spirit usually in response to the Word of God. Whenever you hear an anointed word from God (full of the supernatural power of the Holy Spirit), whether through a sermon, prophecy, song, or reading the Bible, it should bring a conviction if it touches your issue. The Bible says that the Word of God is sharper than a two-edged sword. It cuts to the soul and the spirit, and will identify what is in your heart (Hebrews 4:12, KJV). If a true word from God comes forth, it will bring conviction.

A word from God will convict you while you are on the dance floor at the club, while you are sitting on a bar stool, while you are in the middle of a sexual act, or even mid-sentence while you are saying something that you probably shouldn't say. You may be drunk, high or otherwise influenced, but when God speaks something inside your heart, you will feel like it has been cut, and it will let you know that you are not where you are supposed to be, nor doing what you are supposed to be doing.

If you are not feeling any conviction about your behavior, it may be that at this time, God is not calling you. It could be possible that you have rejected His call for so long, He has stopped wrestling with you. It is a dangerous thing to be doing wrong and never feel any conviction. In some rare cases, it could mean that you have been turned over to a reprobate mind. That means that you no longer have an opportunity to turn things around, and you live life with no conviction of any wrongdoing. It means that God has decided not to argue with you anymore. This is described in the first chapter of Romans. No more calls. No more changes. You are never going to change your mind, so God no longer gives you the capacity to do so.

I am confident that you do not fit that category. This book is for those of you who do not want to stay this way. You know you have behaviors, emotions, desires, habits and/or addictions that have to stop, yet you have no idea how to stop them. If you are convinced, then now you just need conviction. Ask God to give you a conviction about it. Ask Him to send you a word, to speak to your heart, and to infiltrate your spirit. Ask Him to prick your heart over it. Pray, and fast, and read the word. Listen to sermons on the subject and talk to other believers.

My hope is that what you have read so far has helped, and perhaps you feel that conviction now. Even better, I hope that you already had it before you started this book. If not, stay before God until you feel the pain of conviction over this issue. Pray until there is a prick in your heart so that you can honestly tell God that you are sorry for the behavior, and you do not want to engage in the behavior any longer. Pray even now, asking God to forgive you, cleanse you, change you, and help you to feel the regret. Pray until you feel you are truly tired of living with this sin, this issue, this behavior, and you are ready to stop. Do it before the consequences of your behavior make you more sorry than you could ever imagine being. Don't wait until the love of God has no alternative, but to let your repetitive destructive habit have its way with your life. Find the conviction before the heart attack, the vehicular manslaughter, the divorce, the incarceration, the AIDS status, or the bankruptcy. There are ways to truly be sorry for your sins. There are ways to feel a deep regret that are not so pleasant. Maybe you are reading this book because you have already gone down that street. So, what we need is *conviction*. Do you have that? Now, on to the next step.

CHAPTER 3

Conversion
Have You Been Changed?

James was devastated. His wife, whom he loved intensely, had been visiting her parents over a long weekend. On the Friday she left, he had an extremely stressful day and longed for the comfort of his wife, his best friend, to sooth and nurture him through the much-needed three days off. But, she was gone and the long weekend was before him. He went home to an empty house, and the old demons began to call to him. He went to his secret stash and pulled out his favorite DVDs. He watched pornography all night, which he believed satisfied his physical need for release and his emotional need to be relaxed and cared for.

He woke up Saturday morning with a call from his wife. The feeling of conviction was so strong, she could hear it in his voice. She was angry. They had prayed about this and agreed that it was over. She wouldn't even finish the conversation. When she so abruptly hung up, James felt a combination of anger, frustration and condemnation. "She doesn't have a clue about what I'm going through," he repeated to himself. "She is no help. That's not what I need right now." His body began to tug at him. His mind played the night before all over again, but then a new memory came to him, and he was just angry enough with his wife to do it. He got dressed, got into his car, gassed up, and hit the road for a long drive to another city where no one in his circle would run into him. He found that old familiar place where men go to escape into lust and self-gratification. He watched the women dance, and let his mind drift into fantasy. He thought to take things further, but the Holy Spirit convicted him so strongly that he stayed frozen in his seat. He did not leave, but he did not go deeper down the road he knew so well from before he married the love of his life.

Early Sunday morning, much too late to make it back for church, he drove home in torment. He was devastated at his behavior, and really wanted to run as far from the presence of God as he could. Once he was home, the feeling of hopelessness and sadness drove him back to his pornographic movies until he was sick of himself. There was a revival service that night, and even though he dreaded facing the presence of God, he was driven to go to church, almost out of a need to punish himself.

The sermon ironically was about the grace of God and God's desire to free us from the bondage of sin through loving us back to wholeness. His conviction led him to the altar that night. The love of God, and His willingness to forgive and cleanse, overwhelmed him. He collapsed at the altar, and another Christian brother began to do spiritual warfare, miraculously calling out and casting out every demonic spirit that had attacked James over the weekend. And then...it happened. James felt the Spirit of God rush through his human spirit, filling him with power and a new resolve. He seemed to literally feel something break inside of him, and the joy only a free man could imagine burst forth. He was changed, and he knew it. The desire, the lust, the anger, and the frustration was gone. As he drove home, the thought of pornography, or anything sexual that was not his wife, turned him off completely.

He called his wife and reported his experience. She was skeptical and still angry. She believed it was over before and had been disappointed one time too many. They argued and hung up. The thought to go back to the DVDs came rushing up, but even in his emotional state, he wanted no parts of it. He was changed. He had experienced a conversion.

So you feel conviction; now you need conversion. The first group of people Peter preached to were pricked to the heart. They felt conviction. Later Peter preached to another group of people and talked about conversion. In Acts 3:19, through the Holy Spirit, he says, "repent therefore, and be converted." Conviction should lead to repentance, and repentance to conversion. Repentance, remember, is that change of heart, mind and direction about the wrong you have done. Now you are ready to walk in that new direction. You must be converted. Conversion is an inward change at an even deeper level. It is something that God has to do. There are some things God has to pull you out of, but other things God has to pull out of you.

It's like the children of Israel coming out of Egypt. God worked many miracles to pull them out of Egypt. Then came the long process of pulling Egypt out of them. At the first sign of fear, discomfort, confusion, or difficulty, they longed for the things that were familiar, even though slavery was attached to them. When we have not experienced an inward conversion, we tend to revert to the things that previously enslaved us. We find it difficult to stop because although we have repented, we are not converted.

There is much talk about *process* in the Christian world these days. I can admit that for many of us, just like the children of Israel, there is a process before the change is complete. This book, in fact, describes a process that is not only biblical, but one I have found to be successful in producing permanent change. However, I do want to make it clear that a long process is not God's best. God is able, through the Holy Spirit, to do an instantaneous conversion. Today. Right now. If you have the faith to believe it, and the willingness to receive it, the thing you want to stop can be stopped right now!

From this sentence on, you can be free from that behavior. I believe that with all my heart, and I have seen God do it time and time again. The rest of this book can simply be maintenance for you. So stop and ask God to do it in you right now (and then keep reading for some good information on how to help others, as well as keep your change). Here is a prayer to help you along:

Lord Jesus, I believe that it is your will to completely change me and free me from this behavior. I need a conversion in my inner man. I repent of my repetitive, sinful behavior and I renounce it. It is not good for me, and it is not your will for my life. I have the faith to believe that it is over right now. I receive freedom in the Name of Jesus. I give you permission to come into my heart and pull this issue out of me. I thank you for setting me free from this very moment on. In Jesus' Name. Amen!

If you accept that, and believe that, then congratulations! Walk in freedom from this day forward. But, I suspect that if you are reading this book you have prayed about this issue over and over again, and have not experienced instantaneous freedom. I still know God is able to do it that way, but for many of my personal issues, instant freedom has not been the case. So now, let's talk further about conversion and the other steps to gain and maintain your freedom.

To convert something means to alter the nature of it. Conviction, with repentance, changes the way you think about your wrong doing. Conversion alters your very nature. That sin is no longer second nature to you. To convert also means to change from one form to another. To be converted is to be transformed. "Trans" means across or to move across. So, transform is to move across from one form to another. To be converted then, is to be changed, altered, and transformed. Conviction is not enough. It is not enough to feel bad about it. It is not enough to change your mind about it. If you really want to stop you need to be converted.

Conviction without conversion just equals condemnation. You feel bad about who you are, but you continue to be the same person. It causes depression and fear and a sense of failure, which can lead to discouragement, continued failure, and ultimately loss of hope.

Often, this is the predecessor to backsliding altogether, meaning that the person makes the decision to walk away from God and just give in to the behavior, accepting it as his or her lifestyle.

Conviction without conversion will either cause you to live a life of excuses, or give up on God altogether. Failure shakes your faith and makes you wonder if this born again religion is real at all. It causes some people to abandon the biblical doctrine of holiness and adopt one that assumes God does not mind our constant misbehavior because of His grace and mercy. That reaction is nothing new. Paul dealt with it in the early church when he wrote, "Shall we continue in sin that grace may abound? God forbid!" (Romans 6:1) Conviction without conversion is dangerous and destructive.

So then, conviction affects the mind and heart, but conversion affects the nature. Sinful behavior is just not you anymore. This bad habit is not a part of who you are anymore. According to 1 John 3:9, "no one who is born of God will continue to sin, because God's seed remains in him. He cannot go on sinning because he is born of God." Being born again, or born of God, changes your nature so that you can't just go on sinning, and be comfortable and okay with it. You can't even enjoy it. Your outer flesh may crave it, talk you into it, and feel pleasured and satisfied from it, but your inner man, the real you, can't stand doing things that God hates.

It's the God in you, in your spirit that is born of God, that can longer live with the behavior. Many people who continue living in sin, or living with those destructive behaviors, habits, and attitudes, have never been truly born again. They have never been converted. They may have come to the altar, or to the front of the church, said the words they were told to say, and joined the church according to the instructions they were given. But, anyone who walks out the same sinner they were when they walked in, is not truly born again. You need to be converted.

Perhaps, you were convinced. Perhaps, even convicted. Yet, the true test of whether you have been born again is being converted. You have to have a change in your sinful nature. When your mind, heart, and nature have changed, that unwanted behavior will eventually stop. You cannot live with it anymore. Its presence in your life is a nuisance, a speed bump, and an irritant. It may still feel good to your flesh (that nature you had, and the person you were, before being born again), but your spirit, the real you, the newborn you, is so over it! Your spirit does not want it and is grieved by it. If you are honest with yourself, that is why you picked up this book. Perhaps, you picked it up because someone else is grieved about your behavior and handed you the book, but you are reading it because somewhere inside, you don't want to live the rest of your life with this issue. Whatever the reason, at this point ask God for conviction and conversion. Pray that prayer right now. The same prayer from earlier in this chapter, or one that is more specific to the fact that you have been convicted, but not converted. Pray it until you feel it. In my personal conversion I wasn't too proud to beg because I wanted—really wanted … no, I NEEDED to stop. When a true conversion happens there will be a multilevel transformation.

> I beseech you therefore brothers, by the mercy of God, that you present your body a living sacrifice, holy and acceptable to God, which is your reasonable service, (or act of worship). And be not conformed to this world, but be transformed by the renewing of your mind. (Romans 12:1)

> Though the outward man is wasting away, yet the inward man is being renewed day by day. (2 Corinthians 4:16)

> He saved us, not because of the righteous things we had done, but because of His mercy. He saved us through the washing of rebirth and renewal by the Holy Spirit whom He poured out on us generously through Jesus Christ our Savior. (Titus 3:5-6)

There is a renewing that takes place in this process. There is a renewing of the *mind* that is accomplished by studying and meditating on the Word of God. The mind is reprogrammed by truth. When your mind is renewed, you begin to see things like God sees things. So when it comes to that thing you want to stop—you don't *like* it anymore. You see it as the sin it is. You cannot continue to let it be a part of your life. You cannot excuse it, laugh about it, or even think it is fun or cute. You don't like it. Your mind has been renewed.

There is a renewing of the *soul*. When the soul is renewed you do not *need* it anymore. The soul is the seat of your emotions, feelings, will, and desires. Sometimes you have a "soul tie" with that issue. You need it. You need it to cope, to feel normal, to feel safe, or calm, or secure, or nurtured. You need it to feed yourself or to feel alive. All those are soulish needs, but when your soul has been renewed, you no longer *need* it.

Then there is a renewing in your *spirit*. The essence of your very nature. The real you. The God conscious part of you. When your spiritual nature is changed, you do not *want* it anymore. You are a new person on the inside who only wants to please Christ. There is a renewing available at every level of this process, and you need to experience it at every level. We know it is possible to want something you don't even like. You can need something you don't even want. You can like something you know you do not need. So you need God to give you a multilevel conversion. You need to experience a renewal at every level if you have any chance at stopping this behavior. When God renews your *mind,* you don't *like* it. When God renews your *soul,* you don't *need* it. And, when God renews your *spirit,* you don't *want* it.

So, you need *conviction*. You have to have a deep prick to the heart that the thing you need to stop is wrong. That will lead to a true repentance rather than continuous failure followed by repeated apologies. Then, you have to have *conversion*, a change in your nature, an inner transformation, an act of God through the Holy

Spirit. This should come with being born again, but if you do not feel it strongly, you can pray for a conversion. What you may need is a conversion specifically in the area you are struggling. I have asked God for conversion in one area when I had already experienced conversion in several others. So we have *conviction* and *conversion*—but wait, there is more.

CHAPTER 4

Connection
Are You Connected to Your
Source of Strength?

Amber was on fire for God and progressive in her personal life. It was about time! She wasted her 20's chasing love and playing around with destructive habits. Then one day, a near death experience drove her back to the God she abandoned in her college years. During her time away from God, she found ways to swindle, sell, manipulate, and run scams with the best of them. She never got caught, which she thought was a monument to her intelligence. But, when one of her deals went bad, the victim of her scam tried to kill her. Realizing that grace was running out, she cried out to God. At that point, she felt a strong conviction. As her victim pleaded with her to return the money she illegally swindled, she was finally face to face with the pain that her dishonest lifestyle caused real people. She was not an intelligent business mind, she was a thief, plain and simple; regardless of the intricate ways she figured out how to do it.

When her life was on the line, she prayed to the God she had avoided for years. He spared her life, and when she was in a safe place, she cried out to Him again in conviction and repentance, and He performed a conversion in her spirit, soul, and mind. She rededicated her life and hit the ground running. She finished her college degree, got her Master's in Business Administration, and was hired at a prestigious company. God gave her favor and she had skills. Amber was now living the life she was meant to live. People who were seen by her before as easy marks, were now people she loved to minister to, give to, and help in any way she could. She filled her life with work and ministry at a frantic pace and was happy to do it. As time went on, however, she began to notice her temper getting short at home and at church. Her passion for both began to subside. Church was just another stressor, and the people with whom she surrounded herself were all needy, and draining. Passion was replaced with resentment, and the desire to help people be better morphed into a desire for people to leave her alone.

Then it happened. An opportunity presented itself that was almost too good to be true. It was a business deal that would pay off tremendously. The only problem was that it would take some swindling to pull off. It wasn't quite a clean deal. It would use her manipulative, deceptive skills, and it would be a challenge; but, the risk of bad consequences would be extremely low. She would get away with it, and she knew it. She was excited again. A feeling she had not felt in a long time. It was familiar. It was the chase and the challenge of a good con. For some reason, the conviction about doing it was barely there. It was overridden by the excitement. So she went for it and pulled off the deal of a lifetime. Her boss was thrilled, and she was promoted. With the promotion came a bonus she could not have imagined years ago. As she sat in her new office and looked at her bonus check, a coworker came by and said, "I thought you were a total fanatic Christian, but I see you still have some game in you girl—high class, but still a thug for life."

The coworker went away laughing, but Amber felt a deep prick in her heart. She had slipped back into the woman she used to be. What happened to her conversion? Why didn't the Spirit nudge her more strongly? How could she go so far and not feel anything about what she was doing? It would seem that in her prayer time, and in her worship, the Holy Spirit would have said something. Yet, when was the last time she had her prayer time or really went before God's throne in worship? Somewhere she had lost her connection.

Once you have been convicted and converted, you have a new nature. This new nature lives in the old body, and the old body is still used to the sin or the issue you have been struggling with. Usually, that behavior brought some kind of pleasure to the body or the emotions. Moreover, the physical and emotional feelings of the body are in close alliance with the old self, also known as the flesh, which is that person you were before conversion. The flesh is your old mind, old feelings, old habits, and the urges and cravings of the body that are not aligned with the will of God. The old self is always gearing up for a comeback. It is gearing itself up right now, even as you read this book. So you have to be able to gain and maintain power over your old self, your flesh, by staying connected.

The connection is with the Holy Spirit. It's imperative that you learn how to walk in the Spirit. Now, this is where I got irritated in the church. When I was struggling with behaviors I didn't know how to stop, they kept telling me that if I would walk in the Spirit, I would not fulfill the lust of the flesh. That is scripture, I must admit. It is found in Galatians 5:16. That is the answer. Unfortunately, no one was able to tell me exactly how to do that. I won't leave you hanging, though. It is absolutely true that if you walk in step with the Holy Spirit, and maintain that connection, you will be able to stop.

So, to walk in the Spirit you must first be filled with the Spirit. Being filled with the Holy Spirit happens after conviction and conversion. Only people who have been converted are candidates to be filled with the Holy Spirit. Jesus said, in John 14:17, that the world could not receive the Holy Spirit because they do not know Him. Believers can receive Him because we know Him and He will live within us. So if you are not able to continue in the change you want to make, ask God to fill you with the Holy Spirit.

The filling of the Holy Spirit is not just for those who consider themselves Pentecostal in denomination. Every believer in Jesus Christ needs to be Spirit-filled. We may differ on our interpretation of what that means, how that happens, and what happens next. We can even differ on exactly when it happens, but we all know Jesus said we would receive power after it happens (Acts 1:8) and that the Holy Spirit guides us, teaches us, and helps us live according to the will of God (Acts 14:26). You need God to fill you until you feel strong, until you have power, and until that power flows like living water (John 7:38).

In times of temptation, struggle, and testing you are going to need a connection with the Holy Spirit or you will not be able to stand. Do you know why? It is because the demons assigned to you spend all day trying to get you to go back to your old habits. They have nothing else to do. Sometimes that makes me angry. I used to ask God, "How am I ever going to beat the enemy? He doesn't have anything else to do. I have so many other things to focus on, there is no way I can keep up with his strategic attacks against me."

The demons assigned to you will trick you, set you up, and strategize against you. And remember, they have been at it a lot longer than you have. They are better at this than you are. They know you better than you know yourself. They set you up because they know what you will fall for. The enemy knew you would go for that, even when you are shocked yourself! Most of the time, you have fallen for the same trick before. He keeps using the same stuff against you because the same stuff still works.

When you are filled with the Holy Spirit you have special Intel, or intelligence, if you will. What the military calls "Intel" is that inside information that gives them prior knowledge of what the enemy is planning. The Central Intelligence Agency will use spies, secret agents, phone taps, internet scanning, double agents, infiltrators, bribes, bugs, secret recordings, and cameras, all to gather invaluable information. Intel to our military works so that no matter what the enemy does, no matter what they plan, no matter what they strategize against us, we already know about it, have a counter strategy, and the power to thwart the plan.

The Holy Spirit, in connection to our spirit, is that internal intelligence. The Holy Spirit will tell you what your enemy is up to. He will tell you not to go out tonight, not to pick up the phone, where to be, and what time to avoid trouble. The Holy Spirit will not only tell you what to do and what not to do, but the same Spirit gives you the power to obey the direction you have been given, even when parts of you really want the opposite of what the Spirit is saying.

This is why God was able to tell Isaiah to let His people know that He not only made the material that the weapon is made of, but He also created the guy who made the weapon. So God can say without hesitation that no weapon formed against you will prosper (see Isaiah 54). God is saying that there is no strategy that the devil can come up with that His Spirit cannot lead you through successfully. If you stay connected to the Holy Spirit, and walk in step with Him, you can and will stop your sinful and destructive behavior.

So, how does this work? Romans 8:13 says, through the Spirit you mortify the deeds of the flesh. You get up in the morning and walk in the Spirit, meaning that now you live from the inside out. When you feel that tugging on the inside, when that Intel begins to download its information, you obey that inward tugging where the Spirit lives in you, instead of obeying the sinful part of your nature that tugs at your body or emotions from the outside. You obey the inside voice instead of adhering to the outside voices calling to you.

Those outside voices are from the demons assigned to you. Those demonic voices are there to keep you in the struggle with those bad habits and sins. Your own flesh also has a voice that you hear as cravings and desires and urges. So when temptation comes, you will feel the inward tugging of the Spirit to not comply. You will also hear other voices calling you to indulge, and you will feel urges from your body to comply with the demonic voices. Your job is to simply choose to follow the inward tug. It is not easy, but it really is simple.

The Spirit lives inside of you and speaks to you what is right; what to do or not to do. The sinful part of you speaks to you and tries to get you to continue to do the wrong things you are trying to stop doing. You, your mind and your will, now have to make a decision. Walking in the Spirit, or in step with the Spirit, means that you make the decision to do what the Spirit leads you to do. Very simple. You tell one yes and the other no. If you say yes to the Spirit every time, you have now stopped that behavior. Simple... but, not so easy.

How do you get your mind and will to consistently make the right decision? The answer is in the strength of the connection between you and the Holy Spirit. The stronger and more constant your connection to the Holy Spirit, the more likely you are to obey the Spirit in times of temptation. The tug of the Spirit will be strong and overwhelming, and since your mind has been renewed, you really don't like the wrong behavior anymore anyway. Since your spirit has been renewed, you really don't want to do the behavior, and since your soul has been renewed, you certainly don't need to do it. All of that is made stronger and more consistent when you stay filled up and connected to the Holy Spirit.

The problem is that most of us only experience the Holy Spirit in small shots. During a church service on Sunday, or maybe a weekly bible study or prayer service, we take in the Spirit like a shot instead of like being hooked up to an IV (intravenous). When you are determined to stop, you have to stay connected to the Holy Spirit like an IV is connected to a very sick patient. You have to take the Spirit in daily. It has to be continuous.

For example, you turn on some kind of sermon, or do a scripture reading, first thing in the morning. You put Christian music on in your car, or listen to a sermon, all the way to work or school. You take all the music from your favorite secular artists out of your CD player or IPod, and replace it with music and words that feed your reborn spirit. You shut down the radio music that feeds your flesh, and you only play what feeds your spirit. You put your television channels on Christian stations instead of your movie channels, and situation comedies, and police dramas.

You allow time throughout your day for praise, worship, and prayer. You fast several times a week (meaning that you refrain from food and non-spiritual activities for periods of time) to just focus on building up your spiritual life through studying the bible, praying, and listening for God. During these times, you look for God to share with you direction and to fill you with His strength. You do whatever it takes to stay connected to the Holy Spirit. Fill yourself with Him and maintain a constant flow into your human spirit. It doesn't mean that you never participate in any non-spiritual activities ever again. How much feeding of your spirit you need to do depends on how spiritually sick you are.

The bigger your problem, the more powerful your connection needs to be. Just like with the IV example we spoke of earlier. The sicker the patient is, the longer they have to stay on an IV. If there is a little fever, a little infection, you go to the doctor and they give you a shot and some pills to take every day for a few days. But, when you have an infection that has interrupted your body's function, and is spreading throughout your body, they lay you down and put in an IV so that the healing medicine pumps into you all the time. Some issues in your life may have become so severe, so interruptive to the function of your spiritual life, that you will need a spiritual IV. Stay connected. This is the single most important factor in maintaining your freedom once you have been convicted and converted, and the behavior has initially stopped.

To be honest, no matter what your issue is, stopping is not the problem. We do that every day. We do that every night when we fall asleep. Every time we are with people we do not feel comfortable doing our thing in front of, we stop. We stop to work, and travel, and care for others. None of us engage in that behavior 24 hours a day for

7 days a week. We can stop, but staying stopped is the problem. We pick it back up, either the first chance we get, or when the cravings return, or when we are tempted, or stressed, or tired. To stay stopped, there must be a connection to the power of the Holy Spirit and an ability to stay in step with His directions. Again, this is the single most important factor in maintaining freedom.

The connection, then, feeds your reborn spirit. A well-fed spirit will have an easier time dominating the old nature. An old poem I read early in my quest to control and end my own problem behaviors went like this:

Two natures beat beneath my breast.
The one is foul, the other blest.
The one I love, the one I hate.
The one I feed will dominate.

Having a constant connection with the Holy Spirit is achieved by feeding your newborn spirit on a constant basis.

If you are deep in struggle with this behavior or issue, may I suggest going on a feeding frenzy? When the old nature tries to assert itself, sometimes you have to overfill yourself with spiritual things. Take a period of time where all you focus on is feeding your spirit, while starving your flesh. Overdo it on prayer, worship, music, and reading the bible. Double or triple your spiritual activities. Read only spiritual books. Watch only spiritual programming. Keep yourself surrounded by spiritual friends. This will give a booster to your connection with the Holy Spirit and make it stronger.

You should hear the voice of the Spirit more clearly and powerfully. You should be keenly aware of His presence with you daily, talking to you, guiding you, leading you, and helping you make decisions. You will feel the power to obey the leading of the Spirit. You will hate disappointing the Holy Spirit because you will be so closely connected to Him. In order to stop this unwanted behavior, you must have a constant connection to the Holy Spirit.

Next, you will need a constant connection to the source of your strength. This will be different for different people. You have to figure out what strengthens you personally. A better way to understand this is that each person has a particular way in which they access the power of the Spirit more readily. For some people, it is prayer. When things get difficult, and you feel off-centered, prayer may be the thing that always gets you back on track and in the mood to fight again. For others, it may be praise. Turning on your favorite song of celebration, or giving God thanksgiving, or singing, or dancing, or clapping your hands before the Lord may be what kindles your fire.

Perhaps its worship—just being in the presence of the Lord in humble adoration—that sets your attitude right and renews your perspective. It could be a word from God—reading, or hearing preaching, or the scriptures, or a fresh revelation from a scripture you have read before. Maybe a totally different and new fresh word from God is what excites you, turns the fire back on, and renews your strength. Another source of strength is people. Being around a brother or sister in Christ for motivation, affirmation, or accountability. Even coming to a church service where all of it comes together—fellowship, scripture, praise, worship and prayer—may be your key.

You must find your primary source of strength and stay connected to it. How do you typically access the power of God? Moses accessed the power through his staff. Elijah and Elisha had the mantle. Samson's strength came through his hair. David had a harp, a prayer garment, and a slingshot. Daniel's was consistent prayer and fasting. Jesus got away from everything and everybody until He felt renewed. Jesus also got refreshed by doing His Father's will and finishing His work. How do you access the power of God most effectively? What makes you strong? You need to stay connected to your source of strength to keep your power over the temptation to return to what you have stopped.

Then, you need to stay connected to the Body of Christ. In other words, you need to stay connected to your local church. Ephesians, chapter 4, teaches us that if we are connected to the Body of believers, we will mature. We build each other up. Each person in the Body supplies strength to the others in the Body. So then, if you get overtaken in a fault, or get caught up in a sin, the others in the Body will restore you. Not condemn you, not talk about you, not tell everyone in the church, or the family, what you did, but they will restore you. How does this work?

If you stay connected to a ministry leader and spend the afternoon on a church project, you will not be out having sex, getting high, or gambling your paycheck away. Not because that person is stopping you, but because you will not go there if you are with them. You would not invite them to engage in those activities with you because of the respect you have for them. As long as you and that leader are connected, you don't even want to engage in that behavior. If you are hanging out with your pastor all day, it is pretty certain that you won't be buying drugs or picking up a prostitute (assuming your pastor doesn't have the same issue). You may be completely addicted to something, but if you never leave your pastor's side, you will not be using that day. I'm not saying that this is feasible; I am just making the point that all of us stop our inappropriate behavior in the presence of people we really respect who will keep us accountable for our behavior.

So, if you are with a ministry leader on Saturday, and in church on Sunday, and with church family after church on Sunday, you may have enough strength to go to work all day Monday and get through the night. If not, maybe you take a bible class, or get in a small group meeting on Monday night. Then, work all day Tuesday, and work on a church project with other believers on Tuesday night. Wednesday after work, meet with a ministry leader, do bible study at the church, or participate in a rehearsal. Thursday, maybe you go to dinner with several members who get together for fellowship. Perhaps Friday, you are back to the church project, and Saturday, feeding the homeless.

Of course, if you are married and/or have a family those evenings are taken up in family responsibilities, and hopefully you have family support not to indulge in those behaviors. The point is, a week has gone by and your connection to the Body of Christ has kept you out of trouble all week long. That seems like a whole lot of church activity. It is a lot. How bad do you want to stop?

This extreme is for a behavior where you are experiencing constant relapsing. If your problem is not as severe, then a more balanced participation with other believers would be effective. To stay stopped, however, you must have connection with other believers at some level. It is too easy to relapse in private, but very difficult to relapse in public.

Of course, you cannot be with someone from the Body of Christ 24 hours a day, 7 days a week, and 365 days of the year; but, you still have the other connections to help you in between. The connection with the Holy Spirit will strengthen you until you can get with your church family again. That IV of the Spirit will be pumping into you continuously day and night, especially in the midst of the temptation. Staying connected to your particular source of strength will ensure you have very few weak moments. If you have all three of these connections—the Holy Spirit, your personal source of strength, and the Body of Christ—you can, and will, win this battle. You can, and will, break this habit. You can stop.

Conviction—conversion—connection...and then there is *correction.*

CHAPTER 5

Correction
What Are You Still
Doing Wrong?

Jackson was a real man. He was strong, masculine, intelligent and assertive. He was what others would call the Alpha male. Tall and handsome with a muscular build, he was a star athlete in high school and college. He graduated with honors, married the most beautiful and successful woman in his class, and embarked on a career in upper management at a Fortune 500 company. Jackson was the man. He loved his family, and was especially close to his father, who was an Alpha male from the old school. His father was a firm authoritarian and, by today's standards, was physically and verbally abusive.

To Jackson, however, he was the epitome of strength and masculine dominance. He admired the man. His toughness is what made Jackson achieve, and because the results were good, Jackson felt the method was good. So he became mean like his father. He was rude and dismissive at home. He required perfection from his children, and would often withhold affection and kindness from his wife if she did not bow to his will.

As time went on, one of his now teenage children tried to

commit suicide. In her devastation, his wife finally said to him what she had held for so long. She told him that his abusive perfectionism was destroying their family, and she would not allow her children to continue to live under this tyranny. If he did not change, she was going to take her children and leave. Jackson called everyone in that night and found that all the children felt the same way, but had been too afraid of him to have ever told him how unhappy they were.

Jackson was hurt and, most importantly, convicted. For the first time, he sought God for help. He prayed that night in a way that he had not felt the need to since he was a child himself. He had done well without God, but now he remembered the God he learned about growing up in church. That Sunday, Jackson went to church alone. He heard the sermon that Jesus was a problem solver. He had a problem. He was sure of it now. He felt convicted, and after the prayer, he was converted. He brought the family to church the next week, and they all accepted Christ.

Everything was better for a while. Jackson was calmer and more easily entreated at home. He found that prayer was his best connection to maintain his more positive behavior. Still, whenever there was a problem at home, and the children did not line up with expectations, he would revert to his old behaviors. He was a new man at the everyday interactions, but his ideas about discipline, and the withdrawal of affection, never changed.

After a particularly stressful week at work, he came home to rooms in disarray, dishes in the sink, and several below average report cards. He immediately attributed it to his newfound Christianity softening him up too much. It was right to be a Christian and he had no regrets, but this nice way of parenting and running his household was not working for him. He went back to all of his old ways and though he felt a conviction about it, there was nothing else he knew to do to keep his family together. After several weeks of him being a tyrant, he came home to an empty house. His son was back in the hospital on the verge of another suicide attempt, and his wife left him a note that she was done.

Without even finding out where his family was, he found his pastor and sat down for an emergency session. After an hour, they discovered that the problem was that he still held in high esteem the image of his father. His father was his idea of masculine strength. Until his pattern of reverting to this image was challenged in his mind, he would never be able to maintain the change he was trying to make. The pastor suggested ongoing counseling to challenge his thinking, and perhaps even help him discover what he had never been willing to face: the fact that his father was not the great dad he had convinced himself that he was.

He would have to deal with the days he was abused, and recognize that he decided to become an abuser instead of remaining the abused. He would have to see how the abuse affected every aspect of his life, and how he was driven to perfection so that he would not suffer the humiliation his father subjected him to. He would have to see how he placed that burden on his children, and how that contributed to their unhappiness. He needed to be corrected to be free from his abusive ways.

You have to be willing to be corrected. There is usually something in your lifestyle that is supporting your habit or behavior. You must be willing to have those things identified and corrected. When you slip back into a behavior you were trying to stop, there is usually something you are not doing correctly. There is no failure in God, so the failure has to be in you. Maybe there is a door still open that you are not aware of, meaning there may be an unresolved issue that makes it easy for you to fall back into bad habits.

Until you find that issue, and close that door, you are vulnerable to that behavior reoccurring. There may be a thought, or a stronghold from the past, that you haven't dealt with yet. These things sometimes may not even be identified until you fail. Until you mess up, or slip back, you may not even know the issue is there. So, once you find out there is an issue, you must be willing to accept some correction.

Correction may take many forms. One form of correction is called a "breaking." A breaking is when God allows internal and/or external circumstances to literally turn your life upside down. You are broken down so completely you will not know who you are. Everything you leaned on, depended on, and thought you knew, is suddenly shattered. Sometimes, it is a loss. Sometimes, it is a challenge of your faith and belief in God. It could be a betrayal, or an abandonment. It may be the loss of a dream, or a deep depression, or a serious illness.

Whatever God uses, when you are in a breaking, you are most likely the most miserable you have ever been in your life. Sometimes, God can't get destructive things out of our lives until He breaks us down. No one can help you when you are in the hands of God and He is breaking you. A breaking is a private interaction, rather confrontation, between you and God. When you finally come out of it, you are changed forever. It's like Jacob with his limp. The bible says that Jacob wrestled with an angel all night long until the angle touched his thigh and it came out of joint. Jacob was blessed after that encounter. His life was never the same. His name was changed to Israel, but he walked with a limp the rest of his life. Then there is Nebuchadnezzar with his seven-year insanity. He had the wrong attitude about God, and in his breaking, God allowed him to literally lose his mind. After seven years, Nebuchadnezzar had a totally new outlook on God. When you have been broken you will never be the same. It is a form of correction.

Being broken brings you down to what is really important. Sometimes, it makes you so sick of your behavior that, after the breaking is over, you cannot bear the thought of having anything else to do with it. Sometimes in the breaking, you lose all the fight you have and you just surrender to God with a "whatever" attitude. You've wrestled with God, and yourself, and everything you ever thought about yourself, and you somehow come out with a totally new attitude. You have been brought down to nothing and now you have to wait for God to rebuild you into whatever He wants. It is painful, but quite effective. The Bible says, in Hebrews 12, that no correction feels good at the time, but it does have righteous results.

If you are in the midst of the most horrible time in your life to the point that you have no fight in you, and if you have lost every crutch and don't seem to have any options except to take whatever God wants to do, you may be in a breaking. In your breaking, God will begin to correct things that are so deeply ingrained in you, the only way to correct them is to break you down to nothing. The 12 step programs may call this hitting rock bottom. For the Christian, however, this form of correction is not the result of the culmination of your bad behaviors. For the Christian, a breaking is carefully calculated by God to get optimal results. It would be a book in itself to fully explain breaking and there are some books already written on this subject. Suffice it to say, if God is breaking you, there is nothing anyone, or you, can do.

I will guarantee you this: if God is in this process, you will stop the behavior, when it is over. So relax into the process, as painful as it is, and let God finish what He has begun. He is a masterful surgeon, and He knows how to cut from you the sinful cancer that is killing you. He will let you be hurt before He will let you be lost. So, one form of correction is breaking.

Sometimes correction comes with a strategy. If you have difficulty stopping a behavior, there is a way to learn from your mistakes. If you feel a conviction, have a conversion, maintain a connection, and there is still failure or relapse, there may have to be a corrective strategy to keep you from returning to the behavior. Most of the time, that behavior has been intertwined into your lifestyle, so it will take a lifestyle change to maintain your freedom. Correction has to include changes to your lifestyle. Not just changing the target behavior, but also changing all the surrounding habits that made the behavior easy to maintain.

Each time you slip back into the behavior you want to stop,

you have to examine what led to the relapse. How did you mess up this time? What were the steps? What were the missteps? What happened right before? What were you feeling? What was the devil saying to you? How did the enemy talk you into it? What did you say to yourself? Did you miss your way to escape? What was your opportunity to get out of it? The bible says that with every temptation there is a way to escape. A corrective strategy shows you how to identify that way of escape and take that exit.

When we return to our habits or behaviors, we are not particularly fighting against the power of the devil. The bible says we are fighting against his strategies. Ephesians 6:11-12 instructs us to put on the full armor of God so that we can take our stand against the devil's schemes. The devil doesn't have any power against you. All he has is strategy. He knows how to talk you into stuff. He knows how to set you up. He has been around you so long, he knows how you think. Again, the bible says that no weapon formed against you will prosper. We get excited about the part that it will not prosper, but we overlook the fact that it is "formed" against us. I believe that just like each of us have angels assigned to us, we have demons assigned to us as well. They are there to stop us from progressing in Christ, and ultimately to destroy our lives, our souls, and our bodies. Along with that, the enemy plans to take our destiny. To break habits and change behavior, we must have a corrective strategy that cancels out and/or counteracts the strategy of our enemy.

You may need counsel from someone like a pastor, spiritual mentor, or even a professional who can help you figure out how the devil gets in and how to shut him out. You need someone to help you see why you got that midnight call, why that person showed up when they did, and why it happened to be the worst day of your year when they did show up. Then you have to be willing to be corrected. Now is not the time for arrogance, embarrassment, or independence. If you are going to maintain freedom, there must be correction.

Here is how it could possibly work. You are addicted to food to your own physical detriment. Health issues have made it a life and death situation, and the diet and exercise has begun. Staying on the diet is a challenge. You keep slipping up, even though it is killing you. You don't know how to stop. So, now is the time for a corrective strategy. By examining your patterns, you find out that you always give in to your cravings by Thursday night of every week. After talking it out, you realize that the staff meeting you have every Thursday is such a source of stress that, by the end of Thursday, there is no energy to keep on your diet. Furthermore, the food seems to calm you down and gets you through Friday which is filled with the extra work that was handed down on Thursday. Then the weekend lack of structure and frustration from the job increases the need to eat for comfort. Sunday gives more spiritual strength and the diet starts back on Monday.

So the correction strategy is to find a better solution to the stress problem on Thursday. There needs to be something in place so the stress can be handled without food. Either have some better food alternatives available, or engage in an activity that substitutes for the food. You may need an accountability partner that knows to check with you every Thursday after the meeting. You may need to do all the above. Then, add some structure to your weekend. Put in a non-food reward for making it through Saturday. Whatever the plan, it is put together to counteract the plan of the enemy.

Maybe your issue is sexual. You have trouble being faithful to your wife. You examine what happened last time you were unfaithful. It started with being burned out. Then, you met someone whose conversation was exciting...just something different. You let the conversation get intimate and flirtatious just for the fun of it. Then, after an argument with your spouse, you don't resolve it right away. You end up shutting down on your spouse and opening up more to the other person. The abstinence from your marital intimacy increases the desire for the outside relationship. The opportunity presents itself, and you have cheated again.

So the corrective plan can be at any of those levels. When you start to get burned out, plan a vacation quickly with your spouse. You can have an accountability partner ready to share when an interest starts in another person. This person will keep you accountable to appropriate conversation, or even total separation from the person if that is possible. Counseling with your spouse may be a strategy to solve any communication problems so that there is never a shut down after a disagreement. It may be that to keep yourself from going back into adultery, it is never acceptable to not be intimate with each other no matter what the argument. Then, examine how the opportunity presented itself and figure out where there was a way you could have escaped. Develop a plan to make sure you take that exit the next time—very early.

You may be a person who cannot have any friendships with the opposite sex. Your spouse needs to have all of your passwords, along with access to your mail, and email, and phone, and Internet connections to make sure these friendships don't develop. For any corrective plan to work, you really have to want to stop. Correction only works when there has been conviction, conversion, and connection, and you are really determined to stop.

Sometimes, correction takes the form of repetition. God will have you repeat a strategy, or a preventive discipline, multiple times. For example, He may have you go on a fast, and then when you complete that, He may send you on another one. He may have you not watch television and only pray for three days, and when you complete that, lead you to do the same the next week only to increase it to five days. The repetition is designed to develop new habits and break the old ones. The discipline that comes with having to repeat a positive behavior helps to stop the faulty behavior. You end up being way too busy going over to go under.

We have no idea sometimes how deeply the bad behavior or destructive habits are ingrained in every aspect of our lives. The only way to teach an old dog a new trick is by repetition. What it actually does is create new patterns and pathways in our brain. Repeating prayer, and fasting, and abstinence from that habit is also a building up of spiritual strength. Repetition may be God's way of teaching you how to live right, and also empowering you to do it.

Correction may also come in the form of accountability. You need someone you can trust, and who has more spiritual maturity than you do, to know what your issue is and your strategy for stopping that behavior or habit. This can be a pastor, church leader, friend, or family member, but preferably not someone with the same current issue. It's important that you know this person is on your side and that you agree that they have the authority, given by you, to correct you, challenge you, and hold you accountable for your behavior. Often, when leaders have the responsibility of being accountability partners to someone with an issue, the person feels like their privacy is violated. Then when those calls come in, or a behavior is questioned, the person gets offended and insulted.

I ask this question again to those of you who do not want your privacy invaded by an accountability partner; how bad you really want to change? Sin often requires privacy, so if you want so much privacy and independence that you are irritated with the extra eyes on you, then you need to question yourself as to why that privacy is necessary. Is it so that you can have space to fail just in case you want to? If you are going to maintain your freedom and make a permanent change for the better, you must be open to correction, and that will often mean accountability.

Then, there is teachability. When you have an issue that has more of a hold on you than you have on it—when you don't know how to stop—someone who knows how has to be allowed to teach you how it is done. If your counselor, mentor, or church leader gives you an insight or instruction, you must be teachable. If you already knew everything there is to know about stopping this behavior you would have done it already. Just the fact that you are still engaging in the behavior shows that you don't know everything. Evidently, you don't know what to do. Your plan is not working. You have to be teachable. Someone who has more experience can help you lay out a plan that will aid in your long-term freedom. They may just give you a testimony of what doesn't work, and what does, from the perspective of one who has been there, done that, and learned how to stop. Don't let pride and arrogance be your destruction. Be teachable.

Then, there is chastisement. The book of Hebrews tells us that because God loves us, He will chastise us for correction. Chastisement is like a good old-fashioned spanking, or as we called it in my neighborhood, a whoopin' (I think that was the ethnic way to say "whipping"). In this day and time, a whoopin' may be politically incorrect to say, and it certainly is not popular. Some may consider it illegal, but the argument is that sometimes talking to a child does not work. There are those who believe that there are times when a rebellious child needs a good old-fashioned whoopin'. I am in no way suggesting that for your children, but that is what God does to us spiritually when nothing else works and we are bent on destruction. He sent you a word, and it did not help. Your pastor had a talk with you, and it did not help. He sent a prophet to confront you, and it did not help. He let you fall on your face. It did not help. He restricted you. He lifted the anointing (the supernatural ability to minister) from you. He pulled away His presence, and nothing helped. So, now you are a candidate for a good old-fashioned whoopin'.

God does whip His children in His own way. The bible teaches us, in Hebrews 12, that if we do not take correction from God as our Father, then we are bastards, and not sons. The bible says we are illegitimate and we don't belong in His family if he does not chastise us. Good fathers chastise their children, and those children accept it in love. So, if you really want to stop, you not only accept chastisement from God, but also from the ones He has assigned to lead, guide, feed, and nurture you to righteousness. This will mean accepting it when you are asked to take a break from ministry, or go to counseling, or be accountable by checking in and allowing someone into your private world.

The chastisement from God may be a little different than what you may get from a leader. It may be allowing something difficult to happen in your life to get your attention. It may be allowing you to face the negative consequences of your own decisions. Nebuchadnezzar experienced insanity. David lost his child. Cain was marked. Israel was turned over into captivity, but all were better afterward. God will do what He has to do to help you to stop. If you are a son, you will have to endure correction.

Once your lifestyle, or thinking patterns, or emotions have been corrected, you are now on the right path. You are now aware of the things that contributed to your relapses and have developed strategies to counteract those patterns. You have dealt with issues that are open doors for the demons assigned to you, and you have closed them. You have corrected your thinking about the things that supported the behavior. You have had the behavior broken or spiritually beaten out of you. You have been corrected.

Let's review what we have so far. To stop your problem behavior, you must have *conviction*. You must know that the behavior you want to stop is wrong, and have a deep sense of remorse, regret, and sorrow over it. You have to have a *conversion*. God changes your heart, mind, and soul. It is an inside change. You must truly be born again, as well as have a transformation in your spirit about that particular thing. Then you develop and maintain *connection* to the Holy Spirit to continue to have the power, the will, and the strength to maintain your freedom and not relapse back into the behavior. If relapse occurs, or if you find yourself slipping, there must be *correction*. God did His part with conviction and conversion. As long as the Holy Spirit is strong and active in your life there is no reason to fail, unless you are doing something that sabotages your success. That would take some correction. There is now only one thing left.

CHAPTER 6

Conclusion
Are You Done?

I was never really skinny. Obesity was genetic in our extended family, but my mother was a very disciplined person, and although she would have been considered overweight medically, she was much smaller than her siblings. She engrained in her children the discipline of eating right and paying attention to our weight. So, although we weren't a thin family, we were aware, and we didn't go to the extreme. It was in college, when I was away from her control and in the atmosphere of dormitory food, and the cheap unhealthy foods we supplemented our diet with, that the weight began to pile on.

You may have heard of the "freshmen twenty." It is common for college students to gain weight the first year, but mine became the sophomore fifteen, the junior ten, and the senior twenty-five! Oh, then the graduate school thirty and the doctoral thirty-five. Food had become my drug of choice. It was wonderful. It cured everything from my repetitive depressions, to my intense loneliness, to my constant stress. You see, I was a church girl from a strict religious tradition. I lived up to most of the behavioral restrictions (I may never tell the ones that I didn't live up to since I am from Las Vegas, and what happens in Vegas stays in Vegas).

I have never had a cigarette or an alcoholic beverage. I have never been to a house party or went out night clubbing. I am saving my virginity for my husband who has yet to show up. I have never been high and would not know an illegal drug if I saw one. I don't use profanity. I have never had a fight in my life, except some childhood tussles with my younger brother. I don't gamble—not even bingo or a raffle! Yet, my sin was as destructive, and debilitating, and ungodly as them all.

The problem was, most Christians did not believe it. Very seldom was it condemned as sin at church. Being a teacher of the word of God, I have a sensitivity to the accurate interpretation of scripture, and one day I came face to face with the fact that my gluttony was not only sinful, but that it was slowly killing me as it had done several members of my family. Those who were not dead had a very poor quality of life. I was convicted. I read a scripture in Proverbs about deceitful meat. I read in Corinthians about defiling God's temple. I read in several scriptures about excess and gluttony and lasciviousness, and I was *convicted*.

I am not sure how much I was *converted*. Gluttony is a difficult sin because you can't just stop eating altogether. There is no abstinence. There has to be constant control. Although, I heard Kenneth Copeland say once that the alcoholic doesn't stop drinking, he or she just stops drinking alcohol. So I did experience some change in how I ate. I exercised. I lost some weight. I did not keep my *connection* with the Holy Spirit as strong as I should have, however, so every time I experienced a depression, I gained fifty pounds. So, then came *correction*. After an intense suicidal depression, I went to a Christian Psychologist. After taking medications briefly, two years of therapy, and a powerful word from God, my depression was under control. Although it returned from time to time, it was never to that level again. I had an understanding about myself and the patterns that caused my destructive behaviors. I made some corrections and lost weight again.

Again I did not keep my connection as strongly as I should. Nor did I stand fast in the corrections I had made. Working full-time, pastoring full-time, dealing with stress at home, caring for aging parents, and the loneliness that comes with all of that, sent me back to my drug of choice. Food helped me make it through the nights. It helped me celebrate my victories. It filled me up when life drained me. It loved me when no one was there. It gave me comfort and that warm cuddly feeling. It put me in a deep sluggish sleep at night.

Food was my friend, my lover, and my god. I thought of food first thing in the morning and the last thing at night. I was convicted. Not as converted as I would have liked. I was connected, but not consistently. I was corrected, but not following the plan. The problem was—I was not done. There was no *conclusion*.

The health problems began. The inability to move, the fatigue, and the poor quality of life was building. I never did like the way I looked, like most women, but I really did not look well. Not even on Sundays! Older women could out walk me and my joints and back were in pain. I could hear myself huffing and puffing on the recordings of my sermons, and after a day of ministry, I was completely wiped out. I was being convicted repeatedly by my own sermons as I preached about freedom from addiction, and sexually inappropriate behaviors, and character flaws. How could I have counseling sessions with crack addicts, and then go home and indulge in my own drug until I fell asleep?

Feeling helpless, tearful, and ashamed, I finally went to get some professional help. I walked into a Weight Watchers meeting weeping because I was a pastor, and a Licensed Clinical Psychologist, and could not help myself. I didn't know how to stop. I was larger than I ever imagined I would be. I was embarrassed because, during my disciplined times, I gave such passionate sermons about gluttony, and now those who were offended by me were teasing me and throwing my words back at me. I was broken. I was totally defeated. I felt horrible, but as I sat in that first Weight Watchers meeting it hit me. I was done.

This weight was coming off. I was going to change my lifestyle. I was going to fast, and pray, and stay connected. I was going to seek

God for a true transformation. I did not have the words that I am sharing with you in this book because I was living a sermon I had not preached yet, and was writing a book I am just now putting on paper. I was done. Food was not my friend. It was my drug. It was my idol god. It was a murderer, and it was a thief. I still had to eat, but I did not have to worship it. My love affair with food had to be over. It is still kryptonite in my life, but it is not my friend, or my god, or my lover. Our relationship is over. I am done.

Are you done? All the prayers we pray and all the steps you make toward freedom won't do you any good unless you are ready to release the behavior. You can feel bad about it, have the power to overcome any temptation, and have the right strategies to maintain your freedom, but they are null and void unless you are truly done with it. You must bring yourself to conclusion. Are you done?

God is very capable of keeping you from falling (Jude 24). The Holy Spirit will guide you away from temptation, but you have to be done. You need closure. You must say goodbye and mean it. There is a shutdown that happens internally and emotionally when you are done. I learned something about marriage counseling from my mother. She told me she could always tell when a person was done with the marriage and when they were not. If she came to intervene, and they sat down and talked and listened, she knew that no matter what angry things they may say, they were not done. But, when they let her talk and never stopped packing while she was talking, they were done. In my own counseling, I have noticed that when people are not done they will call, ask for advice, threaten to leave and tell me they are done, and I know they are not. When they are really done, they move out, file for divorce, and tell me about it three or four weeks later. They don't want to talk, reason, or explain. There is nothing anyone can say. They are done!

This is what needs to happen to seal the other steps we have written about in this book. Some people have the will power to just hit this stage and never go back to the behavior again. Usually it's because something traumatic has happened, or they have had some other life-changing experience. Being done is certainly one of the most powerful, if not the most powerful, pieces of this process. God has given us the ability to make up our minds. We are free-willed beings. No one but God can make you do what you do not want to do, and He refuses to do that. So I ask you again. As you think about this behavior you have had difficulty stopping, do you see or feel any future in it? Are you really ready to walk away for good? Are you done?

Sometimes we cannot say we are done because we said it and felt it before, and we failed and slipped back into the behavior. I know the pain of that disappointment and how it takes the energy out of your very soul. But, don't let the fear of that overshadow the fact that you are done. That is why the other steps are so important. The demons assigned to you are relentless. Just because you are done does not mean they will not continue to strategize against you. They will wait for a weak day, torment your mind, and make attempt after attempt to get you to fall. This is where conviction, conversion, connection, and correction come in to shore up your decision to quit.

Conclusion speaks to your attachment to the sin or habit. Are you really ready to divorce it and denounce it from your life? Are you prepared to never do it again? Are you done being the person you used to be? Aren't you ready to move on to something else? Something better, something sweeter, something more productive, something more satisfying. Are you done? Can we bring this to a conclusion?

Epilogue

So There It Is

So there it is—a plan that will stop any behavior, habit, addiction, issue or stronghold in your life. You first have to have a *conviction*. You have to believe with all your heart that this behavior is wrong. Not just wrong for you, but against God's will for your life. It has to grieve you.

You have to have *conversion*. The power of God must come into your heart and change you from the inside. There has to be a transformation that is supernatural. God must do it for you and in you. Some things are too ingrained, and too powerful, for you to handle yourself. You need a conversion.

Then there is the ongoing *connection* you must have with the power of the Holy Spirit. He must be in you, live in you, guide you, and strengthen you from the inside. A constant connection with the Holy Spirit is essential to maintain your freedom.

There most likely will need to be some *correction*. Correction is necessary because, for some habits, there has been a lifetime of history between you and the behavior. In addition to that, you have an enemy who is fighting you as well. One habit may be connected to another habit, or an unresolved issue, or an environment, or a person. This must be corrected. You must be willing to be corrected no matter what form that correction may take. Whenever there is a relapse, you ask God to forgive you, examine what you did wrong, and correct it until you get it right.

Ultimately, you have to be done with this issue. There must be *conclusion*. A decision on your part that you refuse to live life with this issue any longer. Your attachment to it is dissolved and you are done. You will stop this behavior. You will break this habit. You will resolve this issue. You have been set free from this sin by the Blood of Jesus Christ. You know how to stop.

Conviction. Conversion. Connection. Correction. Conclusion. When the process has finished its perfect work—you are done.

About the Author Page

D r. Naida M. Parson is a native of Las Vegas, Nevada. She holds a Bachelor of Arts Degree in Psychology and Black Studies from the University of California, Riverside. She has also earned a Master of Arts Degree in African-American Studies, with emphasis in Psychology from the University of California, Los Angeles, as well as, a Doctorate in Clinical Psychology from the University of Nevada, Reno. For over thirty years she has provided and coordinated mental health services for children, adolescents, adults and families.

She has been said to have a prolific and creative "way with words" and has provided motivational speaking for several civil, corporate, and community organizations. She is well known for her ability to reach any audience regardless of age, gender, or cultural background. Her method of presentation causes her audience to look inward and leave the event with renewed enthusiasm and often a plan of action.

Dr. Parson is active in the community as a motivational speaker, writer, and mentor, and is the Senior Pastor of New Antioch Christian Fellowship in Las Vegas. She is a sought after Christian conference keynote speaker. She is the sole proprietor of A Way With Words, LLC, which is the parent company for her speaking, writing, seminars, and training workshops. Dr. Parson is also a Certified Leadership trainer, coach, and speaker.

Printed in the United States
By Bookmasters